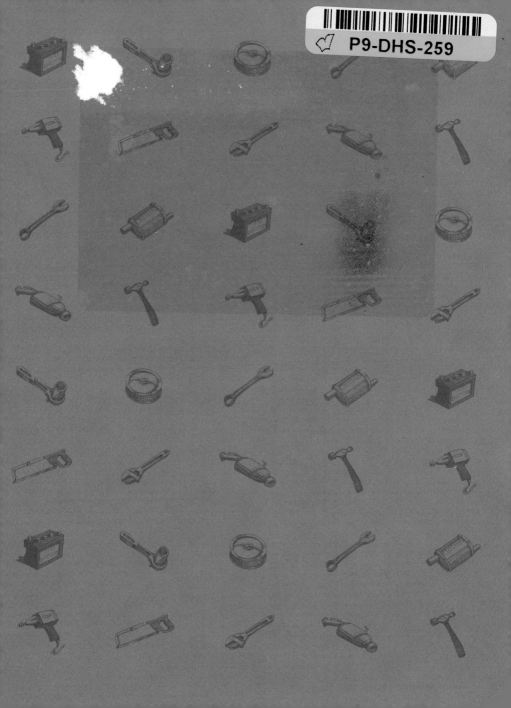

Road Trip Journal & Maintenance Log

CAR TALK

ON THE ROAD WITH CLICK & CLACK, TOM AND RAY MAGLIOZZI

CHRONICLE BOOKS
SAN FRANCISCO

Library of Congress Cataloging-in-Publication
Data available.

ISBN 0-8118-5501-5

Design by Affiche Design, Inc.
Typeset in Albert, Ketchupa, and Rockwell
Manufactured in China
Chronicle Books endeavors to use
environmentally responsible paper
in its gift and stationery products.

Distributed in Canada by
Raincoast Books
9050 Shaughnessy Street
Vancouver, B.C. V6P 6E5

10 9 8 7 6 5 4 3 2 1

Chronicle Books LLC
85 Second Street
San Francisco, CA 94105
www.chroniclebooks.com

See the full range of Chronicle's Car Talk gift
products at www.chroniclebooks.com.

CONTENTS

INTRODUCTION

OVER THE YEARS, WE'VE FIELDED MANY CALLS FROM FOLKS HEADED OFF ON ROAD TRIPS OUT WEST.
Or back East. Or to Mexico, Saskatchewan, or Tierra del Fuego. And we've always encouraged them to stop worrying about what could go wrong—and just go.

What could be more exciting than hitting the open road and seeing the country? Doing all that—and breaking down along the way! A day's inconvenience in, say, Pahrump, Nevada, will lead to a great story (or two, or three) that will last a lifetime and improve with each telling.

While we don't wish a blown hose or leaking radiator on anyone, we hope that if it happens, you'll take it in stride, and remember this bit of time-honored wisdom: The journey of a thousand miles begins with a single broken fan belt.

Don't forget to send photos.

Happy travels,

Tom and Ray Magliozzi
Click and Clack, the Tappet Brothers

It may just be my age catching up with me, but if I were going off to look for America, I'd rent something comfortable and roomy like a Lincoln Town Car. Then if it breaks down in rural Texas, you can call the rental car company and say, "I've got your car here, and I just put a stick of dynamite in the tailpipe. If you're not here in two hours with a replacement I'm gonna light it."

—Tom

TOM AND RAY'S FOUR GOALS FOR DO-IT-YOURSELFERS

Want to spend your weekends covered with grease and cursing softly to yourself? Who wouldn't! Well, here's the most important advice we can give: Your goal is not to fix your car.

That's right. Your first and most important goal is to walk away from your car at the end of the day with all digits, appendages, and eyebrows intact.

Your second goal is not to blow up anything or anyone else.

Your third goal is not to break something that's not already broken.

Your fourth goal is to fix what's broken.

LOOSE BELT
(OR A CAT IN THE ENGINE COMPARTMENT)

CAR TALK TIP FOR A SUCCESSFUL ROAD TRIP

GET YOUR VEHICLE CHECKED OUT.

An ounce of prevention is less expensive than a pound of cure. Or, put another way, do you want to risk passing through the digestive system of wolves because you were too cheap to find a hose clamp before your trip?

We didn't think so.

Make time to get your vehicle thoroughly serviced before you set out. If you need a good mechanic—at home or on the road—you can check our Mechanics Files in the Actual Car Info section of our Web site at www.cartalk.com. (Your laptop will come in handy if you break down on the road.)

It is better to travel in hope than arrive in despair.

—Ray

You can't just figure it out by thinking about it.

—Ray

MYLAR SPACE BLANKET

Will a Mylar space blanket save you at 40 below in blizzard-force winds? Of course not! A good space blanket, however, will reflect back a lot of your heat—they're used by rescuers of all sorts. Having one in your car might just help keep you cozy when you're broken down next January in East Moosejaw, Saskatchewan.

Our humility is what makes us great.

—Tom

TEMPERATURE GAUGE

If your temperature gauge is reading above normal, slow down for a while and see if the needle returns to its usual location. Speed, a heavy load, and extreme heat can cause the engine to run hot, even if nothing else is wrong. But if the temperature does not return to normal at slower speeds, drive slowly to the nearest safe pit stop and have a mechanic check it out. If the gauge gets near "H," or the "HOT" light comes on, it's best to pull over immediately and call for help so you don't do permanent damage to your engine.

CAR TALK ECO-TIP

DON'T TOP OFF YOUR GAS TANK.

When you're refueling, stop when the gas pump automatically turns off. Why? Besides the embarrassing stain on your chinos, overfilling your tank can ruin your gasoline-vapor recovery equipment. The recovery canister is supposed to store gasoline vapors rather than release them into the atmosphere. But if you overfill the tank and liquid gas sloshes into the canister, it will stop working, contributing to the formation of ground-level ozone, smog, acid rain, and airborne toxins.

HEAVY-DUTY JUMPER CABLES

This is one tool you shouldn't skimp on. Why? Because a lot of jumper cables on the market today simply aren't up to snuff. In fact, in our humble opinion, most of them are cheap junk. They're either too short or too thin or won't stay flexible in cold weather—which is when you really need them.

We recommend you buy cables that are at least 15 feet long, which gives you plenty of length to work with. They should be at least four-gauge—thicker, if possible. Finally, they should be made of copper, so there's less resistance.

CAR TALK TIP Make sure the cables you're getting work with the side posts found on some batteries—many cables don't. Check before you buy, and you just might avoid a series of self-inflicted nuclear dope slaps the next time your car battery keels over at 20 below zero.

It's the stingy man who spends the most. And when that happens, the stingy man's wife never lets him forget it.

—Ray

FRONT END: GULLA, GULLA, GLUGLUGLUGLUGLUG

WHAT IS IT?

BAD AXLE ON A FRONT-WHEEL-DRIVE VEHICLE

(OR TOM DRINKING ESPRESSO MACCHIATO)

START SIMPLE.

Start with the easiest repairs first. Don't dive right into rebuilding your transmission. Here are some great repairs for novice shade-tree mechanics, in order of increasing difficulty:

- Change wiper blades
- Replace air filter
- Replace headlight
- Replace battery
- Replace spark plugs
- Change oil
- Replace belts

If you want to tackle a repair that's not on this list, at least make sure it doesn't require you to lie on your back, deep underneath your car.

If you do have to jack up your car to get underneath it, do not use the flimsy jack that came with the car. Never, ever get under your car unless it's supported by approved jack stands. (Unless, of course, you can get your mother-in-law to hold the car up. In which case, we'd like to see photos.)

Sincerity is the most important element of a relationship.
Once you've learned how you fake that, you've got it made.

—Tom

Whatever you do, don't forget to rotate the fuzzy dice.

—Ray

TRIANGULAR FOLDING REFLECTOR

Breaking down on the side of the road is bad enough without a bread truck plowing into you. We recommend you have a sturdy, heavy, triangular folding reflector on hand.

CAR TALK TIP The best kind has a base that's loaded with sand so it won't blow over when that semi comes barreling down the road.

CAR TALK TIPS FOR DOGS AND THEIR OWNERS

SAFETY FIRST

The safest place for your dog to travel is in a crate in the far back, or in the back seat with a dog seat belt. Never have your dog ride in the front passenger seat. And never, ever let your dog drive. Dogs are famous for "accidentally" ending up at the nearest steak house.

As classic an image as it is, veterinarians advise you not to let your dog stick her head out of the window. Even if she doesn't get hit by an errant pebble, dogs do jump from moving cars if the right reason comes along. If your pooch insists on the "window treatment," invest in a pair of Doggles, which provide protection from foreign objects, wind, and UV light. (They're quite the canine fashion statement, too.)

OIL PRESSURE GAUGE OR LIGHT

The oil pressure indicator doesn't measure the amount of oil in your car's engine—unless it's practically zero. It measures oil pressure. And the results of ignoring this gauge can be disastrous. If you keep driving with the oil light on, your car could melt down in front of your eyes in a mile or two.

So we recommend you pull over as soon as it's possible to safely do so, turn off the engine, and check your oil level. If you're lucky, you'll just need to add some oil, since lack of oil can cause low oil pressure. If you're unlucky, you'll be glad you've got that car club membership and the cell phone. There's some possibility that the problem is just a malfunctioning sensor, but let a pro be the judge of that.

CAR TALK COURTEOUS-DRIVING TIP

ARE YOU A TAILGATING KNUCKLEHEAD? READ ON!

Here's a quiz: The tailgating rule is to leave one car length between your car and the car in front of you for each 10 mph you're driving. (For example, if you're driving at 60 mph, leave six car lengths.)

_____ True   _____ False

If you checked "True," you're wrong. Nearly all states have changed to the two-second rule. Here's how it works: Pick a stationary object ahead of you on the roadside. When the car ahead passes that object, start counting off two seconds ("one cappuccino, two cappuccino . . ."). If you get to the object before counting the full two seconds, you're tailgating.

By the way, this is more stringent than the car-length rule. And it works at all speeds. You'll be glad that the buffer zone is there when the transmission falls out of the car in front of you.

Even SUV drivers seem to hate other SUV drivers.

—Tom

You should never let a car interfere with your happiness.

—Ray

MECHANIC'S WIRE

To the untrained eye, mechanic's wire probably looks like just 20 feet of 18-gauge galvanized wire, right? Well, actually, that's all it is. But this little roll of wire is incredibly versatile and will come in handy!

CAR TALK TIP Mechanic's wire is great for reattaching loose mufflers and exhaust parts, wiring trunks shut—or securing anything else that's falling off, like Uncle Harold's toupee.

CAR TALK TIP FOR A SUCCESSFUL ROAD TRIP

TELL SOMEONE IN YOUR FAMILY WHERE YOU'RE GOING.

If you're the kind of person who feels uncomfortable knowing that friends and family members might not able to reach you all the time, e-mail your itinerary to them along with your cell phone number. They'll probably feel better knowing they can reach you.

NEAT STUFF TO HAVE IN YOUR TRUNK

FIX-A-FLAT TIRE SEALANT

Someday, somewhere, you'll be really glad you have a can of Fix-A-Flat in your car. (You can thank us now.) It contains gunk that seals up small leaks, and enough compressed air to get you to a gas station.

If you do get a flat, you'll want to use Fix-A-Flat as soon as possible, before all the air escapes from the tire. Otherwise, the tire may separate from the wheel, and then it won't work.

Oh, and there's one other thing: Fix-A-Flat is not a great dessert topping. Trust us on this one.

CAR TALK TIP If you're in a dangerous place—like the side of a highway—when you get a flat, forget about changing the tire. You can drive on a flat tire. You can't go very fast or far, but you can go. It might cost you a new tire, and it may even cost you a new wheel. But consider the possible alternative: the cost of a funeral—yours.

BATTERY, CHARGING, OR ALTERNATOR LIGHT

If your car's alternator light comes on, it means that your car isn't generating all the electricity it needs. You may have less—and sometimes a lot less—than an hour of driving before your engine shuts down. If the battery light comes on, immediately shut off all accessories, like the radio, air-conditioning, heater fan, navigation system, and electric George Foreman grill the kids are using in the back. Then pull into the nearest gas station and ask them to check your car's charging system.

FRONT END: VWISHHHHHHHHHHHHHHHHHHHH

WHAT IS IT?

VACUUM LEAK
(OR WIND BLOWING THROUGH RAY'S BALD SPOT)

There are definitely benefits to downshifting as you approach a stop sign. It's just that they're not mechanical. They are that 1) you can pretend you're Mario Andretti, and 2) it sounds really cool.

—Tom

DON'T BE ASHAMED TO ASK FOR HELP.

It happens. You got your old serpentine belt off and the new one on—and your car runs backward! (Actually, that's not true. It probably won't run at all.) Don't be shy about calling your regular mechanic. Our advice is to fess up immediately. Tell him you screwed up your repair and need a question or two answered. If he's a nice guy, he'll do it. Don't take advantage, however. Remember your mechanic is probably extremely busy trying to pay off his new 24-foot cabin cruiser.

If you really did manage to "fix it till it's broke" and have to take your car to your mechanic, don't try to cover it up. We can tell immediately when a customer has tried to hide a repair gone awry. Everyone makes mistakes, strips bolts, and breaks off parts. It may take a few decades, but eventually you'll even laugh about it.

VISE GRIP STRAIGHT-JAW LOCKING PLIERS

Vise Grips are the emergency alternative to carrying around a full set of English and metric sockets. In our opinion, this is the most versatile tool you can have in your car. There are all sorts of uses for Vise Grips, including removing stubborn nuts and bolts and tightening battery connections. There are more creative uses for the tool, too. For example, if you have a leaking coolant hose, clamp the Vise Grips onto the hose and temporarily stop the leak. If your alternator bracket breaks, you can hold it in place with Vise Grips. Got bad allergies? Strategically tightened Vise Grips can prevent unsavory spraying of the inside of your windshield and dashboard.

CAR TALK TIP Get the original, sturdy Vise Grips—not cheap knockoffs from Outer Mongolia.

FIRST-AID KIT

We know you've been planning to put a first-aid kit in your car—but you just never got around to it, did you?

Will a first-aid kit stop the bleeding from a slashed aorta? Nope. But you should have a basic first-aid kit on hand so that when you bash your knuckles using those Vise Grips we told you to get (see opposite page), you'll be all set. A good first-aid kit should include a selection of bandages, a few sterile gauze pads and dressings, some antibiotic ointment, acetaminophen tablets, and a pair of nitrile (similar to latex, but nonallergenic) protective gloves.

CAR TALK TIP It's often less expensive to buy these items individually at a drugstore than to purchase a fancy, prepackaged kit.

A problem well defined is a problem half solved.

—Tom

BRING A CELL PHONE AND A BASIC REPAIR KIT.

If you're headed into the remote hinterlands, consider a more powerful, external antenna for your cell phone—and don't forget to bring the charger. However, not all cell phones work where we need them the most: in the middle of nowhere.

Also bring along a basic repair kit for your vehicle, for those fixes you might be able to take care of yourself. At the very least, bring screwdrivers, Vise Grips, and a big roll of duct tape. For a full list of what to bring, see the Roadside Survival Guide in the Actual Car Info section of our lousy Web site, www.cartalk.com.

BACKFIRE
(OR THE RESULTS OF A "SUPER BURRITO" BREAKFAST)

Our car alarm of choice is a Rottweiler. That will deter most thieves, although I'm told it can be quickly defeated by a bucket of extra-crispy Kentucky Fried Chicken.

—Tom

PETS AND ANTIFREEZE DON'T MIX.

Antifreeze is deadly to dogs! Even in small amounts. To make matters worse, traditional antifreeze is sweet smelling and attracts pets. There are brands of antifreeze made from propylene glycol, which is much less toxic to pets than the usual ingredient, ethylene glycol. Some other brands are "embittered," so they don't appeal to pets. Ask your mechanic to use a "pet safe" antifreeze if he has one.

Reality often astonishes theory.

—Tom

NEAT STUFF TO HAVE IN YOUR TRUNK

SAFETY GLASSES

How many of you have a pair of safety glasses in your car? That's what we thought. However, putting on an approved set of safety glasses is the very first thing you should do before you attempt to jump-start your car or start poking around under the hood.

CAR TALK TIP Safety glasses are never in fashion. Remove yours as soon as it's safe to do so.

You learn a lot about human nature when you hand someone a repair bill for $700.

—Ray

DUCT TAPE

Duct tape is great for temporarily fixing hose leaks, repairing busted side mirrors, and hiding rust holes before your annual inspection. Duct tape is very easy to tear in both directions. You can make a piece of duct tape fit just about anything.

CAR TALK TIP Duct tape is also excellent for taping your mother-in-law's mouth shut when she's in the back seat on Day 3 of a 10-day journey. Not that we know anything about that.

CAR TALK ECO-TIP

DON'T USE MORE OCTANE THAN YOU NEED.

Lots of drivers think that they're benefiting their engine or the environment by occasionally "treating" their car to premium gas.

That's hogwash.

Modern engines that don't require premium gas don't benefit from it in any way. And, in fact, most experts say excess octane creates more pollution. So unless your owner's manual specifically calls for the use of premium gas, don't bother. Regular gas is better for the environment . . . and your wallet.

Marriage Advice: Which would you rather be, right or happy ?

—Tom

GOJO HAND CLEANER

Gojo is the official waterless hand cleaner of Neanderthal car mechanics the planet over. This stuff is amazing—after that emergency roadside valve job, it'll get your hands so clean that all your boss will notice at your presentation an hour later is that wonderful citrus aroma you're wearing.

CAR TALK TIP Gojo and many other similar cleaners are now available in single-use packets.

CAR TALK COURTEOUS-DRIVING TIP

LEARN TO FORGIVE (OR CULTIVATE A LOUSY MEMORY).

Forgive others their transgressions. The simple fact is, if we want to reduce road rage, it has to stop somewhere. Our advice? Keep your hand off the horn, and keep your fingers in perfect alignment. Not convinced? Remember this: That guy you're yelling out the window at could work for Tony Soprano.

Spot a really crazy driver? Let the police deal with him. If he's driving like a maniac, chances are he's what? A maniac. Try to get his license plate number, pull over to the side of the road, and use a cell phone to call the cops.

FROM THE TRUNK OR GAS TANK: NNYINN, NNYINN, NNYINNN, NYONNGGG, NYONGGGG, NYONGGG

WHAT IS IT?

BAD FUEL PUMP

(OR TOM PRACTICING HIS SITAR)

DON'T DRIVE 15 HOURS A DAY.

Think your reaction time is just as good at 10 P.M. as it was at 7 A.M.? You're kidding yourself. Professional truckers aren't supposed to drive more than 12 hours a day—and you shouldn't, either.

Even if you're keeping it under 12 hours, it's still important to stop frequently. Take a 15-to-30-minute doughnut break (or tofu break, for the health-minded) and a good stretch every few hours.

CHECK ENGINE

If this light comes on, it is generally not an emergency. All it usually means is that your vehicle's computer has detected an irregular reading in one of the many engine sensors that it monitors. Often, the problem is related to the emissions control system, which can wait until you get to a mechanic. Don't panic.

DO YOUR
HOMEWORK!

Do some research before
you plunge into a repair. It just
might save you a migraine later.
Buy the manufacturer's shop
manual for your vehicle from
your local dealer, and read up on
the repair. You can also consider
signing up for an online account
with Alldata's DIY (Do-It-Yourself)
service, which will give you specific
diagnostic and repair information
for your car. You'll find a link at
www.cartalk.com.

Here's one true story of why it's
important to do your homework:
When we first got involved in car
repair, we once contemplated
a job and took a quick look at
the service manual. It had only
six steps. We decided we'd go
for it, so we went out and bought
the parts. When we looked
at the manual more closely,
we noticed that step 1 said,
"Remove engine." No kidding.

So read the manual!

Remember, it's ONLY a car.

—Ray

98% of all misinformation about cars and driving is passed on by fathers.

—Ray

The other 2% is passed on by us.

—Tom

Just what is "Male Answer Syndrome?" It's the need by men to provide an authoritative-sounding answer despite the fact that they have no idea what the ^&*# they're talking about. Not that we know anything about that.

—Tom

A HOT DOG IS AN UNHEALTHY DOG.

Cars heat up very, very quickly—especially in the summer. Never leave your dog alone in the car. If you see heavy panting and your dog isn't reading *Playdog*, that's a bad sign. Also, glazed eyes, a rapid pulse, bright red gums, unsteadiness, or vomiting may indicate heat stroke. You will need to act immediately to save your pet from permanent disability or death. Move your dog to a shady spot, and pour cool water all over his body. Use ice packs if you have them. Let your dog drink a small amount of water. And get to a vet immediately!

If you're afraid of everything, you might as
well lie down and start throwing dirt on your face.

—Tom

NEAT STUFF TO HAVE IN YOUR TRUNK

OIL RAGS

Having a few clean rags on hand is a great idea. They'll be there when you need them to absorb fluids of all kinds, whether oil, gas, coffee, dog barf, or cerebrospinal fluid. Then again, if you're mopping up cerebrospinal fluid, you have bigger problems on your hands than the stain on your shirt.

CAR TALK TIP Double the number of rags you think you'll need. Then add a few more. If they do get oil-soaked, dispose of them properly to avoid spontaneous combustion.

FROM THE REAR: @#@%!#*&!!!!

WHAT IS IT?
MOTHER-IN-LAW

Never buy a car as an investment. Buy a car to drive. That way, you'll limit your disappointment to only one area.

—Tom

CHECK YOUR AIR PRESSURE BEFORE YOU START DRIVING WHEN ON A ROAD TRIP.

Improper air pressure in your tires can lead to poor handling or, in extreme cases, a tire blowout. Check your tire pressure every day before you start driving, when the tires are cool. If you check your tire pressure during a pit stop, the pressure reading will be higher (and wrong) due to the heat created by driving.

Never let the facts stand in the way of a good story.

—Tom

CAR TALK TIP FOR THE BUDDING DO-IT-YOURSELF MECHANIC

SAFELY DISPOSE OF TOXIC CRUD.

After you're done with your repair, you may be left with used coolant, motor oil, brake fluid, or other toxic materials. Dispose of them safely—and by that, we don't mean dumping it on your neighbor's award-winning Malaysian petunias.

If you ask nicely, your mechanic will likely accept your waste for a proper burial. You may have to pay a small disposal fee. In many states, retailers are required to accept used motor oil, coolant, and other fluids—as long as you have a receipt showing you bought an equal amount of the product at that business.

Finally, you can always surrender your toxic fluids at your local hazardous-waste facility. For information on your town's rules, just type in your ZIP code at www.earth911.org.

FROM THE WHEELS: FLOOVB, FLOOVB, FLOOVB, VWOMP, VWOMP, VWOMP

WHAT IS IT?

BAD TIRE
(OR YOU JUST RAN OVER A MINI)

Our No. 1 rule of driving during snowstorms is: don't. Call in sick and watch television. You'll be one less stranded motorist the rescuers need to worry about, and one more ratings point for "Columbo" reruns.

—Tom

JOIN A
TRAVEL CLUB.

If you're not already a member of a travel club, join one now. It'll save you a hassle when you least need another migraine. There's always AAA. But if you don't agree with their anti-environmental stances, check out some of the other options listed in the back of this journal. In addition, many auto manufacturers offer their own privately branded roadside service.

Why ANYONE is in a rush to get TO work, I'll never understand.

—Tom

NEAT STUFF TO HAVE IN YOUR TRUNK

ROADSIDE-SURVIVAL BAG

Once you've assembled all the neat stuff you need for your trunk, buy yourself a good storage bag. We recommend a dry bag, which kayakers and canoers use. It's very durable and totally waterproof. It'll also come in handy if you decide to run the Snake River in your Kia Rio.

CAR TALK TIP Buy something spacious, with plenty of extra room so you can add items as needed. And check with Martha Stewart to find out this year's must-have color for trunk-wear.

CAR TALK

BINGO

B	I	N	G	O
Booooo-gus	In my humble opinion	Our fair city	Knucklehead	Male answer syndrome
Subway Fugitive	Mike Easter	Picov Andropov	Box 3500	Boat payment
Wasted a perfectly good hour	You can't do it unless the number is two	FREE!	Don't drive like my brother	Vacuum leak
Oxygen Sensor	Bad CV joint	Bullfeathers!	Are you sitting down?	Obfuscate
Sleep in the garage	I like it!	Good luck!	Neanderthal	Stop badgering the witness!

CAR TALK

BINGO

B	I	N	G	O
Bald guy in sports car	Driver on cell phone	Driver picking nose	Speed trap	Donna (Red Camaro with blonde)
SUV with one passenger	Road rage	Jalopy	Construction Zone	Roadkill
Ambulance	Traffic helicopter	FREE!	Roundabout	Car accident
Blue-haired senior	Future roadkill	Breakdown	Soccer mom in minivan	Hitchhiker
Undercover cop car	Vanity plate	Motorcycle momma	Four-way stop	Caution sign

ON THE ROAD

THUNKA, THUNKA, THUNKA . . .
THE CAR TALK GUIDE TO FLAT TIRES

STUFF TO DO BEFORE YOU GET A FLAT

Find Your Jack and Try It Out, Jack

Why? Because when the time comes to change your tire, you can bet your steel-belted radials you'll find yourself on a lonely stretch of highway, in the middle of the night . . . with a raging blizzard in progress. (Did we mention the hungry wolves?) Wouldn't you rather have a little familiarity with all the tools you'll need to change a tire—before you find yourself in that situation?

Ask Your Shop to Please Not Overtighten Your Nuts

Who cares? Well, when the time comes for you to remove the lug nuts . . . you may not be able to. (No kidding—it's possible to make them that tight.) The Goldilocks touch is important here. Not too loose, not too tight.

Don't Bother with a Full-Sized Spare

Unless you regularly drive through Death Valley or down the Alcan Highway, we don't think it's worth lugging around a full-sized spare. Space-saver spares are convenient, easily stowed, and significantly lighter. Over many years of driving, they'll save you a fair bit of cash on gas. They're usually good for fifty miles or so, enough to get you to a gas station in most parts of the country.

The only exception? When you need to show your mother-in-law how little room there is in your car, so she'll have to ride with Uncle Throckmorton.

Consider Replacing the Lug Wrench That Came with Your Car

We've seen a number of lug wrenches that are, in our humble opinion, complete junk. Get the right size socket for your wheel's nuts. For foreign cars, and some domestics too, it'll be a metric wrench. While you're there, buy a nice 18-inch breaker bar, which will give you a lot of leverage to loosen those overtightened nuts.

Do Everyone a Favor and Skip the Wheel Locks

Car dealers love selling wheel locks, which protect against the theft of expensive alloy wheels. Removing them requires a specially patterned socket—which, by the way, is very easy to lose. (Many of them have been lost right at our shop!)

It's very hard, if not impossible, to remove the wheel nuts on a wheel with locks by using a regular lug wrench. It's also very easy to strip the specially patterned wheel lock.

A number of sportier, high-end cars are now coming with "low–aspect ratio" wheels. (The aspect ratio is the ratio of the tire wall height to the width of the tire.)

Here's the catch: They're also very prone to damage from potholes, curbs, and other roadside hazards. To make matters worse, many low–aspect ratio wheels are also aluminum. So what? Well, that could involve several boat payments!

Fix-A-Flat Is Not a Permanent Solution

A can of Fix-A-Flat is a great temporary solution for a flat tire. How does Fix-A-Flat work? It injects a compound that temporarily seals your tire's leak. At the same time, it reinflates the tire. Fix-A-Flat will only work on tires that still have some amount of air pressure in them and whose bead has not separated from the wheel.

Fix-A-Flat is most definitely not a permanent solution, however, and you'll still need to drive right to a garage.

Run-Flat Tires Work

Run-flat tires are designed to do just that. They allow you to drive your car safely for many hundreds of miles after your tire has lost air pressure. They're a great choice if you live in fear of dealing with a flat.

How do run-flat tires work? They have a much stiffer sidewall than conventional tires, and as a result they won't collapse when they lose their air pressure. There is a price to pay, however: Run-flats are about 60 percent more expensive than regular tires, and they provide a stiffer ride.

Another benefit to run-flat tires is that there's no spare tire in your car—which will improve your gas mileage, and leave extra room for smuggling biscotti and cannoli over state borders.

HOW TO CHANGE A TIRE

So You've Got a Flat. Don't Worry About Your Tire. Get to a Safe Location.
Move off the highway immediately. Even with a flat tire, you can drive about 20 mph and still keep your car under control. You can drive several hundred yards before you irreparably destroy the tire.

There Are Some Times When You Just Shouldn't Change a Tire
TIME #1: When you can't safely get off the road—and we don't mean just getting into the breakdown lane. Don't believe us? Try jacking up one corner of your car, and see what it's like when a plutonium tanker whizzes by at 80 mph. The draft will toss your car around like a Yugo in a tornado. That's a lousy time to be crouching next to it.

TIME #2: When driving in the breakdown lane is allowed, which it is—in some of the more moronic states in our nation. (Why is this moronic? Because it's the *breakdown lane*.)

TIME #3: Any time it doesn't feel safe to you, for any reason.

CAR TALK TIP So you're not the kind of person who wants to change your own tire? So what? This is not the New Jersey Turnpike edition of *Survivor*. Get the new, run-flat tires (see opposite page), or join a travel club, or just keep driving (slowly). You'll ruin the tire, and maybe even the wheel, but it's only money. Your life and safety are worth much more.

When you do need to change a tire, and it's safe to do so, here's how:

Find the Spare—And All The Tools You'll Need
Ideally, you already know where these are. If not, you might check your owner's manual. (Remember that? It's that shrink-wrapped, unread booklet that's been in your glove box since you drove your car off the lot.)

Then lay them all out, so you know exactly what you're dealing with. Got a digital camera or a cell phone that takes photos? Snap a couple of pictures of how everything goes back together, and you'll know how to put stuff back when the time comes.

Loosen the Lug Nuts
Using the wrench, loosen the lug nuts, which hold the wheel onto the car. Then finish taking them off by hand. Don't just toss the lug nuts aside. Put them together in one location— your pocket, or a secure place on the ground, preferably away from the nearby precipice, sewage lagoon, or lug nut smelter.

If your mechanic wasn't kind enough to adjust the setting on his impact wrench, you might find the nuts rather hard to get off. Try holding firmly onto your car and pushing down with your body weight.

Jack Up Your Car

Find the correct location on your car to place the jack. Your owner's manual will have a diagram. Expand the jack by hand until it's as tall as it can be and still fit under the car.

Now you're about to raise the car. Unless your name is Vin Diesel, you'll need the jack's handle. Insert it into the jack according to the instructions.

Start cranking. Before you know it, the corner of the car will be off the ground. It doesn't need to be 20 feet in the air—just get the wheel an inch off the pavement.

Remove the Wheel

Take the wheel off and put it down in a safe location away from traffic. Don't put it in the car just yet. (Your car is jacked up, remember? Stay clear of it until it's firmly on the ground.)

Install the Spare

Now it's time to put on the spare. Line the lugs up with the holes in the rim and gently slide it on, being careful not to bang the threads on the lugs. Now loosely screw on those nuts that you sensibly placed in a single safe location. (Remember, it's "righty-tighty," "lefty-loosey"—unless you're south of the Equator.) Tighten them securely, but not with all your strength yet. Then lower the jack and allow the corner of the car to come firmly back onto the ground.

Now comes the fun part! You don't want those lug nuts to come off when you're driving, do you? (We sure don't. We can't afford to lose any more listeners!) Holding firmly onto the car, use your body weight to fully tighten each lug nut. Note that the order of tightening is important. Pick any nut to start with and tighten with the wrench. The second nut you tighten is the one that's "diagonally" opposite. There are two that are sort of diagonally opposite—pick either one. Using the wrench, secure the second nut. The next one to tighten is the one that's (sort of) diagonally opposite from number two. And the next is sort of diagonally opposite from number three, etc., until you've done all five.

Clean Up After Yourself!

Do yourself a favor and don't toss everything in the trunk of your car. Put it back exactly the way you found it, so it's there the next time you need it—and so it doesn't rattle every time you go over a bump and slowly drive you totally bonkers.

HOW TO JUMP-START YOUR CAR (WITHOUT BLOWING IT UP)

YOU HAVE THREE OBJECTIVES WHEN YOU'RE JUMP-STARTING A CAR:

1. Not causing an explosion.

2. Not damaging either car's electrical system.

3. Getting the "dead" car started.

To meet Objective No. 1, you'll need to clearly identify the positive and negative terminals of both batteries. Unfortunately, the markings aren't always as clear as they should be, so you may have to scrape off some dirt or use a flashlight to get a clear look at the marks.

Once you've unquestionably identified all of the terminals, you can proceed to the next step: avoiding an explosion. When batteries explode, it's because a spark has been created in the vicinity of the battery. So the key is to avoid creating a spark anywhere near the battery.

Sparks can only fly when you make the very last connection of the jumper cables and complete the circuit; in other words, when you have three cable ends hooked up and you're attaching the fourth. That's why you want to always make that last attachment in a location well away from the battery. Oh yeah, and this would be a great opportunity to try out those ultra-fashionable safety glasses.

Before we get started, here's one more thing you may need to know: Some newer cars actually have remote terminals for the battery under the hood. The battery itself is located elsewhere. So instead of a battery, you're looking for some large, well-labeled terminals.

SO HERE'S HOW YOU DO IT:

1. First, make sure the "live" car's engine is turned off. We find this cuts down on necktie-in-the-fan-belt syndrome. Although you could start with either car, we're going to suggest you start by taking one end of the red (positive) cable and clamping it securely onto the positive terminal of the "live" car's battery. Be careful not to let the dangling ends of the jumper cables touch.

2. Take the other end of that red cable and clamp it to the positive terminal of the "dead" battery.

3. While you're over at the "dead" car, take an end of the black (negative) cable and attach it to the negative terminal of the "dead" battery.

4. Then, to avoid an explosion, attach the other end of the black cable to some large, unpainted metal part of the engine block on the "live" car—NOT to the negative terminal of the "live" battery. The negative terminal of the battery is simply a ground terminal. By using another, more remote piece of metal to ground the circuit, you can make sure that any sparks that might fly are kept far away from the battery.

5. Make sure all accessories (lights, air conditioner, and so on) are turned off in both cars. Then start the car with the "live" battery and keep it revved at medium speed (about 2,500 rpm) for a few minutes. The alternator of the good car will then be effectively "charging up" the "dead" battery. Then try starting the "dead" car. If it doesn't start, rev the "live" car for five or 10 minutes more and try again.

6. If it doesn't start after that, give up and call for help, because either your battery is stone cold dead or something else is wrong. Continuing to mess around with it at this point is only going to increase the chances of failing to achieve Objective No.1 (page 111).

7. Once the car with the dead battery has started, remove the cables in the exact opposite order that you put them on, again taking care not to create sparks or get your ponytail, ascot, or necktie stuck in the fan.

HOW TO SET YOUR MIRRORS (SO YOU CAN ACTUALLY SEE!)

For years, we'd been setting our side-view mirrors so that they gave us a view of the outside back corner of our cars. This is the way it's been done for generations—from grandfather to father to us! But we finally discovered something very interesting. The back corner of the car never moves. It always stays in the same exact place. So there's really no reason to keep an eye on it.

By moving the side mirrors farther out, you can line up all three of your mirrors so they have minimal overlap—and you can see everything behind you and beside you.

1. KNOW YOUR GOAL!

Here's what you're after: When a car comes up behind you, you should first see it in your rearview mirror. But as it passes you (let's say on your left), you'll see it move to the left side of your rearview mirror. And as its left headlight disappears from your rearview mirror, it should instantly show up in your left side-view mirror. There should be no delay. It should slip from one to the other, so you can always see it.

2. START BY SETTING YOUR REARVIEW MIRROR AS YOU NORMALLY WOULD

Get a good image in your rearview, then lean your head all the way to the left so it touches the driver's window. From that position, set your left side-view mirror so you can see the back corner of your car. Now lean the same distance the other way, and set your right side-view mirror the same way.

3. FINE-TUNING YOUR SIDE-MIRROR ALIGNMENT

You might need to make some slight adjustments to your side-view mirrors to make everything line up perfectly. And pulling up next to a line of parked cars (to simulate another lane of traffic next to you) is a good way to do that.

4. END RESULT? NO HUGE BLIND SPOTS.

Driving with the mirrors this way takes some getting used to. You have to learn to rely on your rearview mirror first. And you'll have to get used to what your side-view mirrors are now looking at. But the good news is that your blind spot should now be gone!

CAR TALK OFFICIAL SUMMER DRIVING TIPS

Here are some things to have your mechanic do before you set out for the Annual Bratwurst Festival in Lower Coleslavenia:

1. CHECK OUT THE ENTIRE COOLING SYSTEM
Radiator, coolant, belts and hoses, cooling fans, heater core, and water pump.

2. TIRES
Check tread depth, uneven wear, and tire pressure. If you're doing the Official 10,000-Mile Tour of Desolate Wastelands, get a real, full-size spare.

3. THE FRONT END
Check ball joints, tie-rod ends, and all other steering components.

4. CHANGE THE OIL
Look for leaks.

5. CHECK THE AIR-CONDITIONING SYSTEM
Refrigerant level, compressor clutch, and belts.

6. CHECK THE TRANNY
Are you close to the recommended service interval? Is the fluid nice and clean? Any leaks?

CAR TALK OFFICIAL WINTER DRIVING TIPS

ANY SMALL PROBLEMS YOU HAD WITH YOUR CAR IN GOOD WEATHER WILL BE BIGGER PROBLEMS IN BAD WEATHER.

If you had the slightest trouble getting old Betsy started in warm weather, you can absolutely count on staying home when the temperature goes "south," so to speak. So what can you do to get ready for the coming glaciers? Here are our tips.

1. If your car needs a tune-up or is due for regular service, get it done before cold weather sets in. Better to fix things at your convenience than after you've been sitting in your car for three hours waiting for AAA. (Just kidding, Triple A! No one has ever had to wait three hours for one of your tow trucks, have they? Naahh!)

2. Make sure your battery and charging system are up to snuff. Your mechanic should check the battery, charging system, and belts. If you find that you need a new battery, get the biggest, meanest, ugliest battery that will fit in your car.

3. Check the cooling system, making certain the antifreeze will protect your car to the lowest winter temperatures in your area. If your coolant hasn't been changed in several years, get the cooling system flushed. If you have leaks, get them fixed.

4. Make sure your windshield wipers are in good shape. Winter wipers—with the rubber coverings that keep ice from collecting on the blade—are great in the winter, but you should take them off in the spring. They're heavy, and if you use them all summer, you'll eventually wear out the wiper motor and the more expensive wiper linkage.

5. Keep your gas tank close to full. If you get stuck or stranded, the engine will be your only source of heat. And you don't want to have to worry about conserving fuel and saving the planet right at that moment . . . you want to stay warm. (Keep a window open a crack if you're sitting there with the engine running.) If there's snow on the ground, make sure your tailpipe is completely clear. If it's snowing, check every half-hour. That's also a good opportunity to get out, stretch, get some fresh air, and admire the scenery.

6. Make sure your windshield washer reservoir is full. Keep some extra fluid in the trunk. Get the good stuff—not the half-frozen blue junk outside your local gas station! Some cheap fluids freeze at around zero degrees.

7. A lot of folks ask us about carrying sand in the back of the car. If you have a rear-wheel-drive vehicle that needs help in the snow, you can put a few bags of sand over the rear axle—that would be somewhere in the trunk. Line it up with the center of the rear wheels. You can make things worse by putting too much weight too far back. If you weight down the rear end too much, you "lift up" the front end and lose some steering and braking ability. Trust us—we're the experts when it comes to carrying extra weight in the rear.

On a front-wheel-drive car, you don't need sand for traction. An enormous weight (the engine, that is) is already over the wheels that are powered. You might want to carry a little sand, though, in case you get stuck on ice.

8. If you live someplace like western Siberia or northern Minnesota, think about adding a block heater to your engine. For less than a hundred dollars, you can be virtually guaranteed that your car will start—even when it's so cold your nose hairs shatter.

9. Make sure your rear window defroster works.

10. Know your car and how it drives in snow. You should know if it has antilock brakes and traction control, how they work, and how they help. In fact, you should practice using these features in an empty parking lot before you have to use them on the roads.

11. If you really have to drive in the snow on a regular basis, get four good snow tires. If you absolutely can't afford four snow tires, two will be better than whatever you have on your car now.

12. Make sure you have some basic supplies in your car in case you do get stuck. Invest in a substantial snow brush and an ice scraper. It's good to have a shovel and a bag of sand to help with traction. A blanket is a good idea—just in case. If you have any winter clothes you don't wear anymore, throw them in the trunk, too. (This is a great place for your old lime-green sweater and plaid woolen pants.) An old pair of boots may come in especially handy. The last item we always carry? Robert A. Caro's biography of Lyndon Johnson. It's 900 pages, so it's sure to keep you occupied until help arrives and beyond. (This can do double-duty as the "weight over your axle" in Item 7.)

13. Driving emergencies are among the few legitimate uses for a cell phone in a car. Just promise us you won't use it while the car is moving, okay? Thanks.

14. If you're in an area that permits or requires tire chains, they should be in the trunk, too. Practice putting them on before you need them. Trust us—applying tire chains is much harder when you're knee-deep in slush in the dark, with other cars whizzing by.

15. Clean snow off your entire car before setting out. This not only enables you to see from all windows (note: snow is opaque), but it prevents big chunks of snow from flying off your roof and blinding the sewage truck driver behind you.

16. When driving in the snow, do everything slowly. Even with good coolant, snow tires, stability control, all-wheel drive, and a bag of doritos in the trunk, driving in snow, sleet, and ice is very treacherous. Do everything slowly and gently, leaving plenty of distance between you and the other cars.

17. If you're thinking about a new car, think about safety features that will help you in lousy weather. If you really have to drive a lot in the snow, all-wheel drive is a good option. If you drive in the snow a few days a year, front-wheel drive is fine.

MAINTENANCE AND MORE:

TAKING CARE OF YOUR CAR

CHANGING THE AIR FILTER

THE AIR FILTER STOPS AIRBORNE CONTAMINANTS—DUST, LEAVES, WAYWARD PELICANS, AND SO FORTH—FROM GETTING SUCKED INTO YOUR CAR'S ENGINE.

It's important to change your air filter, because if it gets too dirty, your engine won't be able to suck enough air into the combustion chambers. The engine will run rich (i.e., too much gas and not enough air). Your car will lose power and run roughly, and your Check Engine light may come on.

If you really neglect the air filter for a long time, your car may stop running altogether. It's pretty tough to do permanent damage to your engine this way, but it is possible.

If you frequently drive on dirt roads or do a lot of stop-and-go driving, you should inspect and replace the filter twice as often as recommended.

INSPECTING THE BRAKES

YOUR BRAKE PADS AND/OR SHOES PRESS AGAINST THE ROTOR OR DRUM ATTACHED TO YOUR WHEELS, CREATING FRICTION AND STOPPING THE CAR—IDEALLY, BEFORE YOU HIT A CABBAGE TRUCK OR A ROADSIDE FIREWORKS STAND.

Brake lining wears down over time. If you neglect your brake pads and/or shoes, your brakes will ultimately fail. Even before that happens, you can cause damage to other, more expensive brake parts, such as rotors, drums, and calipers. In other words: a stitch in time . . . saves you from bringing wheelbarrows of cash to your mechanic later on.

KEEP AN EYE OUT FOR THE FOLLOWING SYMPTOMS WHEN YOU BRAKE:
- flashing brake warning light
- squealing, chirping, or grinding noises
- pulsations in the brake pedal
- shaky steering wheel
- increased stopping distance
- car pulls to one side when you stop.

If you experience any of these, your brakes may require servicing. Make an appointment with your mechanic right away.

CHANGING THE COOLANT

COOLANT, WHICH IS COMMONLY CALLED ANTIFREEZE, IS A FLUID THAT ABSORBS HEAT FROM THE ENGINE AND THEN DISSIPATES IT THROUGH THE RADIATOR.
It also sends heat through the heat exchanger in the passenger compartment to warm your tootsies in the winter.

Coolant is a mixture of ethylene or propylene glycol and water, usually in a 50/50 ratio. It's important to change your coolant, because certain coolants will break down over time, and all coolants eventually lose their rust inhibitors. In time, bits of rust will clog the tiny passages within the radiator and heater, causing your engine to overheat. The result is a bonus yacht payment to your mechanic that someone else should be making.

If you check your coolant level when the engine is cold, the coolant should be at or above the "minimum" or "fill" line on the transparent refill container. If you check it when the engine is hot, the coolant should be at or just below the "max" line.

If you live where the temperature dips below freezing, ask your mechanic to check the concentration of the coolant. Coolant that's too diluted or weak can freeze when the temperature drops below 32 degrees Fahrenheit.

Look in the owner's manual to see if your car uses "long-life" coolant. If it does, check with your mechanic to see when it should be changed. Some "long-life" coolants will last as long as 100,000 miles, but a number of these new coolants haven't performed to expectations and need changing much sooner. When in doubt, change your coolant—it can never hurt. Regardless, it's a good idea to periodically check the coolant level. It's always possible that your cooling system has developed a leak.

INSPECTING THE CV BOOTS

THIS IS THE RUBBER COVER THAT PROTECTS THE CONSTANT VELOCITY JOINT ON FRONT-WHEEL-DRIVE CARS AND A FEW WITH REAR-WHEEL DRIVE.

The rubber boots degrade over time and can crack or tear open. The grease that the boots hold in will then leak out, exposing the CV joint to dirt, moisture, and dead possums. Eventually the joint will fail. Replacing the CV joint can cost hundreds of dollars, whereas replacing a boot costs a fraction of that amount.

Car Talk Tip When you get your oil changed, ask your mechanic to check the CV boots while your car is up on the lift. It'll take him or her less than a minute.

INSPECTING THE DRIVE BELTS

EVERY CAR HAS A WATER PUMP, A POWER-STEERING PUMP, AND VARIOUS ACCESSORIES—ALL OF WHICH ARE POWERED BY RUBBER DRIVE BELTS.

On older cars, each of these components is driven by its own belt. On most modern cars, they're all driven by one belt called a serpentine belt.

Belts need to be inspected and changed, because they eventually wear out. If your car has individual belts and one of them breaks, whatever part that belt was powering, such as the alternator, power-steering pump, or water pump, will stop working. If the serpentine belt breaks, all of these parts will stop working. Engine damage may result from overheating.

In between service intervals, inspect your car's belts for cracks. If you hear a screeching noise coming from under the hood—especially when you start your car on a cold morning or when making a sharp turn—you probably have a loose belt.

REPLACING THE MOTOR OIL AND FILTER

CHANGING YOUR VEHICLE'S OIL IS ONE OF THE MOST IMPORTANT THINGS YOU CAN DO TO AVOID BRINGING LARGE BAGS OF MONEY TO YOUR MECHANIC.

Owner's manual recommendations for oil and filter changes vary from 3,000 to 10,000 miles. We recommend that you change them every 5,000 miles.

YOU MAY WANT TO CHANGE YOUR OIL MORE FREQUENTLY IF:

• You drive like a knucklehead. You know what we mean: jackrabbit starts, heavy acceleration, or high speeds.
• You live where the climate is extremely hot or cold.
• You often drive on dirt roads.
• Your engine is old and burns oil.
• You frequently carry heavy loads (several mothers-in-law or other cargo).

Why bother changing your car's oil? Well, oil undergoes thermal breakdown due to high operating temperature. When this occurs, the oil becomes less effective as a lubricant. Parts of the engine rub together and wear out.

Also, oil absorbs water, dust, and combustion by-products and holds them in suspension. Eventually, the oil gets saturated with this junk and can't absorb any more. Then that stuff stays in the engine and can cause accelerated wear of bearings, cylinder walls, and piston rings.

GET IN THE HABIT OF CHECKING
THE OIL LEVEL EVERY FEW HUNDRED MILES.

With your car parked on a level surface, remove the oil dipstick, clean it on your brother's best shirt, and then reinsert it. Remove it again and check the oil level.

Ideally, it should be right at the full mark. If it's at or below the add mark, that means you're a quart low and should add a quart of oil to the crankcase. If it's in between the two marks, you can add part of a quart to bring it up to the full mark. (The distance between "add" and "full" represents a quart, so use that to estimate how much of a quart you need.) Since oil flows slowly when it is cool, the dipstick may not immediately reflect any oil you just added. So estimate the amount you need based on your first dipstick reading, and then check it later that day or the next day to be sure you're near the full mark.

Be careful not to overfill. If you put in too much oil, the engine's crankshaft can actually come in contact with the oil, quickly whipping it into something resembling a frothy oil cappuccino. Why is that bad? Well, it's not tasty, plus the oil pump can't pump froth very well. Thus, oil doesn't get to the parts of the engine that need lubrication. This could result in you signing your next paycheck directly over to your mechanic.

If you regularly run low on oil, be sure to report it to your mechanic. You may be leaking or burning oil.

CHANGING THE POWER-STEERING FLUID

POWER-STEERING FLUID IS THE HYDRAULIC FLUID THAT TRANSMITS THE POWER IN POWER STEERING.

Over time, the seals, O-rings, and internal power-steering components will wear out. When they break apart, they contaminate the power-steering fluid, which forces the power-steering pump to work harder and eventually break down. When that happens you may also damage the power steering rack, which will require you to take out a small home-equity loan to replace.

If you hear a whining or moaning noise when you turn the steering wheel, you should have your power-steering system checked. Your power-steering pump may be about to fail. (If the pump is okay, the whining may just be your kids asking for an advance on their allowance again.)

Also, if you notice a leak of any kind, make sure you keep the fluid topped up.

REPLACING THE SPARK PLUGS

SPARK PLUGS ARE LITTLE DEVICES THREADED INTO THE CYLINDER HEAD THAT TAKE IN HIGH-VOLTAGE ELECTRICITY AT ONE END AND CREATE A SPARK AT THE OTHER END.
The spark ignites the gas and air mixture to power the car.

Spark plugs do, eventually, wear out. Every time a spark plug fires, it loses a tiny bit of metal from its tip. Also, your spark plugs can get "fouled" or become coated with burnt oil, which would indicate that you have a more serious engine problem.

If you don't replace your spark plugs, your engine will eventually start to misfire and run poorly, efficiency will decrease, and emissions will dramatically increase. Your car may also be difficult to start. In other words, you'll be driving something that sounds and acts exactly like one of Tommy's junkers.

We recommend replacing the spark plugs at the manufacturer's recommended interval.

INSPECTING THE TIMING BELT/CAMSHAFT DRIVE BELT

THE TIMING BELT ALLOWS THE CRANKSHAFT TO DRIVE THE CAMSHAFT, WHICH IN TURN OPENS AND CLOSES THE VALVES.

Without this belt, the engine can't run, period. Checking your timing belt for wear or looseness will let you know if the belt may likely break soon or if it may possibly jump a notch.

If you don't periodically inspect your timing belt, it might break at an inopportune moment—like when you're trying to pass a furniture truck on a two-lane road.

Many modern cars have interference engines, or motor wreckers, as we in the trade refer to them. If a timing belt breaks or jumps a notch in an interference engine, the valves may open at the wrong time and then be struck by the pistons. The result will be many hundreds of dollars in damage to your engine. Be sure to ask your service technician if your vehicle has an interference engine.

If you don't have an interference engine, a broken timing belt will leave you stranded but won't do any permanent damage.

If you hear a slapping sound coming from your engine, it could be the result of a loose timing belt.

CHECKING TIRE PRESSURE

IT'S A GOOD IDEA TO GET IN THE HABIT OF CHECKING YOUR TIRES' AIR PRESSURE AT LEAST MONTHLY, IF NOT MORE FREQUENTLY.

Why? Because having the proper tire pressure is a crucial safety issue. If tire pressure is too high, then less of the tire tread touches the ground. Your car will bounce around on the road, and your traction and stopping distance will suffer. Your ride will also be less comfortable. (If you notice that every tie you own has coffee on it, check your tire pressure. It may be too high.)

If the pressure is too low, then too much of the tire's surface area touches the ground, which increases friction between the road and the tire. Not only will you get poorer gas mileage, but your tires will wear prematurely and could overheat. That can lead to tread separation—and a nasty accident. One sign of low tire pressure is that your tires squeal when cornering.

You need to check your tire pressure even if your tires aren't leaking. Why? Because it changes with the temperature. Tire pressure decreases by about 1 pound per square inch for every 10-degree drop in outside air temperature. So if you last checked your tire pressure in July, when it was 80 degrees outside, and it's now January—and 20 below—your tires may be underinflated by 10 pounds, which is dangerous.

How do you determine the correct pressure for your car's tires? Don't go by the number on the tire. That's the *maximum* allowable air pressure. The recommended pressure is almost always lower. Check your owner's manual to find out where recommended measurement is noted. It's usually printed on the driver's door pillar or the glove compartment door, or sometimes on the gas filler door.

Get an accurate tire gauge. The popular pencil-style gauge is notoriously inaccurate. Analog, dial-type gauges or digital gauges tend to be fairly accurate.

You should check the tire pressure when the tire is cold—i.e., when the tires have been sitting for a few hours or haven't been driven for more than a few miles. Check all four tires—and check the spare at least once in a while. If you have a space-saver spare, then the pressure should be printed right on the spare.

When you bring your car in for service, ask them to check the tire pressure; most garages will do this at no additional cost.

CHANGING THE TRANSMISSION FLUID

TRANSMISSION FLUID ACTS AS A LUBRICANT FOR ALL OF THE MOVING PARTS INSIDE YOUR TRANSMISSION.
In an automatic transmission, this fluid also serves as a coolant and a viscous fluid that transmits power from the engine to the transmission.

Automatic transmissions use something called—shockingly—automatic transmission fluid. Manual transmissions use a variety of oils (but definitely not automatic transmission fluid). Your owner's manual will tell you what kind of fluid to use, and how often to have it "freshened up," as Martha Stewart would say.

Automatic transmissions generate enough heat to degrade and break down the fluid over time. In a manual transmission, the fluid doesn't break down so much, but it gets contaminated over time as the synchronizers, bearings, and gears in the transmission wear out. The resulting metal particles then float around in the lubricant, where they shorten the life of your transmission.

In between service intervals, it's important to regularly check the transmission fluid level. Letting your car run low on transmission fluid can cause the transmission to shift improperly—or not at all. It also can harm your transmission.

If your car has an automatic transmission, it'll probably have a dipstick for this purpose. But not all cars with automatic transmissions do. Don't make the common mistake of confusing the transmission dipstick with the crankcase dipstick. Check your owner's manual to find out the correct procedure.

Checking the transmission fluid in a manual transmission and some automatics can be difficult. A few thoughtful manufacturers have included a dipstick, but that's the exception rather than the rule. If your car has a manual transmission, we suggest that you ask to have the fluid level checked when your mechanic has your car up on the lift to change the engine oil.

CAR TALK TIP Unlike engine oil, transmission oil doesn't burn up. So if you're low on transmission fluid, you almost certainly have a leak.

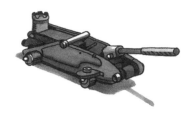

If you've found these tips as useless as
we have, you can post a question
on one of our *Car Talk* bulletin boards:
www.cartalk.com/board. Or e-mail Tom
and Ray for their newspaper column:
www.cartalk.com/email/email.

Still feeling stumped? Trust us,
we know exactly how you feel—we get
that feeling every weekend, for about
an hour.

In the event that you want to do a
little more research into a car question
or conundrum, here are some good
resources. We hope they help more than
we would!

CAR SHOPPING AND CAR SAFETY

CAR TALK
Test Drive Notes, Guide to Auto Safety, Used Car Pricing, New Car Research, Classifieds, and our unique *Car Talk* Car Survey with information from more than 200,000 *Car Talk* visitors.
www.cartalk.com

NHTSA
Recalls, safety info, complaints, crash tests.
www.nhtsa.dot.gov, 1-888-327-4236

INSURANCE INSTITUTE FOR HIGHWAY SAFETY
Vehicle ratings, crash tests, safety research.
www.iihs.org, (703) 247-1500

JD POWER
Consumer satisfaction ratings.
www.jdpower.com (click on Consumer Site: Auto)

CONSUMER REPORTS
Car reviews, car buying guides (subscription required).
www.consumerreports.org

MECHANICS

CAR TALK MECHANICS FILES
A database of mechanics recommended by *Car Talk* listeners.
www.cartalk.com/content/mechx

COMPLAINTS

COUNCIL OF BETTER BUSINESS BUREAUS AUTO LINE
Mediates disputes over vehicles still covered by a warranty.
www.lemonlaw.bbb.org

AUTOMOTIVE CONSUMER ACTION PROGRAM (AUTOCAP)
Another mediation program between customers and dealerships.
Contact your local dealer association.

CAR TALK
Contact information for all the major auto manufacturers.
www.cartalk.com/content/features/To-The-Top

MORE INFO

AUTO CLUBS

AAA
Roadside assistance, trip planning.
www.aaa.com

BETTER WORLD
Roadside assistance, trip planning, environmentally friendly advice.
www.betterworldclub.com

MILEAGE LOG

DATE OF FILL-UP	ODOMETER READING	GALLONS PURCHASED	MILEAGE / NOTES
/15/06	68132	21.2	miles traveled / gallons = MPG

DATE OF FILL-UP	ODOMETER READING	GALLONS PURCHASED	MILEAGE / NOTES

DATE OF FILL-UP	ODOMETER READING	GALLONS PURCHASED	MILEAGE / NOTES

MILEAGE LOG

DATE OF FILL-UP	ODOMETER READING	GALLONS PURCHASED	MILEAGE / NOTES

DATE OF FILL-UP	ODOMETER READING	GALLONS PURCHASED	MILEAGE / NOTES

DATE OF FILL-UP	ODOMETER READING	GALLONS PURCHASED	MILEAGE / NOTES

DATE OF FILL-UP	ODOMETER READING	GALLONS PURCHASED	MILEAGE / NOTES

MILEAGE LOG

DATE OF FILL-UP	ODOMETER READING	GALLONS PURCHASED	MILEAGE / NOTES

DATE OF FILL-UP	ODOMETER READING	GALLONS PURCHASED	MILEAGE / NOTES

DATE OF FILL-UP	ODOMETER READING	GALLONS PURCHASED	MILEAGE / NOTES

DATE OF FILL-UP	ODOMETER READING	GALLONS PURCHASED	MILEAGE / NOTES

DATE OF FILL-UP	ODOMETER READING	GALLONS PURCHASED	MILEAGE / NOTES

REPAIR & SERVICE LOG

DATE	ODOMETER	SERVICE / NOTE	COST
7/5/06	68452	oil change	$45

DATE	ODOMETER	SERVICE / NOTE	COST

DATE	ODOMETER	SERVICE / NOTE	COST

DATE	ODOMETER	SERVICE / NOTE	COST

DATE	ODOMETER	SERVICE / NOTE	COST

DATE	ODOMETER	SERVICE / NOTE	COST

NOTES

NOTES

NOTES

STUFF TO REMEMBER TO TELL (OR ASK) VINNIE
NEXT TIME YOU BRING YOUR CAR IN FOR SERVICE

NOTES

STUFF TO REMEMBER TO TELL (OR ASK) VINNIE
NEXT TIME YOU BRING YOUR CAR IN FOR SERVICE

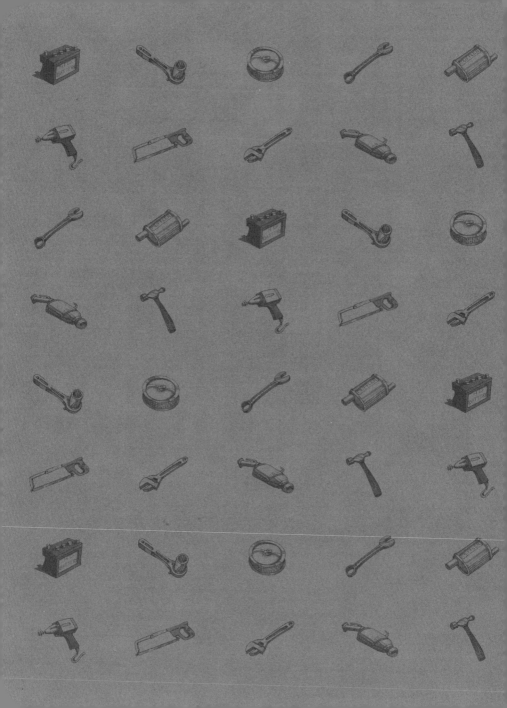